THE FACEBOOK ADVERTISING
FIVE STEP FORMULA
TO GET MORE TRAFFIC

By: Maria Gudelis

For information about special discounts for bulk purchases, please contact vMedio Publishing, a division of vMedio, Inc at (519) 331-7042 or www.MariaGudelisHelp.com.

More great published books by Maria Gudelis:

7 Step Action Plan to Getting Speaking Gigs
The Twitter Business Advantage
21 Ways to Use Social Media

Table of Contents

Why Facebook?

There is a simple reason for you to use the power of Facebook:

> **Because that is where your customers are!**

When you have **HALF A BILLION people using Facebook**, wouldn't you want to participate in the biggest marketplace "on the net"?

FACT 1: Facebook is the largest social community website.

FACT 2: Facebook gets more monthly visitors than any other website except for Google and the numbers are breath-taking – 132 million unique users per month!

FACT 3: One savvy author got traffic of over 2,000 people in less than two weeks after starting her Facebook page

FACT 4: You get "global reach" with Facebook! If you want to attract for instance European buyers to your real estate deal…you can effortlessly! The following graphic from CheckFacebook.com shows Facebook world users.

10 Largest Countries	
1. United States	133,925,380
2. United Kingdom	28,003,500
3. Indonesia	27,800,160
4. Turkey	23,833,140
5. France	19,284,420
6. Italy	16,706,640
7. Philippines	16,675,160
8. Canada	16,465,260
9. Mexico	15,483,640
10. India	13,580,100

FACT 5: More "older" users are hopping on the social media bandwagon. Facebook just isn't for kids anymore. In the U.S., here is a breakdown by age of Facebook users (source: CheckFacebook.com)

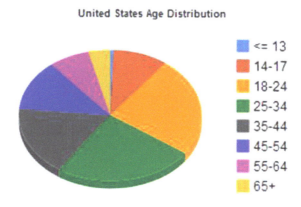

United States Age Distribution

Legend:
- <= 13
- 14-17
- 18-24
- 25-34
- 35-44
- 45-54
- 55-64
- 65+

FACT 6: The trend of "older" users adopting social media is growing significantly! According to a survey by Pew Research Center Social networking use among internet users ages 50 and older nearly doubled—from 22% in April 2009 to 42% in May 2010.

FACT 7: 50% of all Facebook users log into the service each day

FACT 8: The cumulative total of minutes users spend on Facebook each month is 500 billion!

FACT 9: Where U.S. Internet users spend their time online, social media dominated all other categories at more than twice the time spent on the next closest category. Illustrated in the graphic is a Nielson report finding:

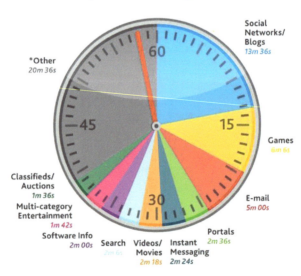

If all U.S. Internet time were condensed into one hour, how much time would be spent in the most heavily used sectors?

Social Networks/ Blogs *13m 36s*

*Other *20m 36s*

Games *6m 6s*

Classifieds/ Auctions *1m 36s*

E-mail *5m 00s*

Multi-category Entertainment *1m 42s*

Software Info *2m 00s*

Portals *2m 36s*

Search *2m 6s*

Videos/ Movies *2m 18s*

Instant Messaging *2m 24s*

Other refers to the 74 remaining online sectors visited from PCs/laptops

nielsen

Fact 10: More than 100 million Facebook users engage with Facebook on other websites each month.

Fact 11: There are more than 100 million active users accessing Facebook through a mobile device.

FACT 12: If you haven't started using Facebook Ads for your business yet, you're missing out on an excellent (and highly targeted) opportunity.

Why Facebook Ads?

 As you can see, you get a HUGE opportunity to reach an even bigger client base than you are reaching right now. The key is to identify who your 'target customer' is…and now you can zero in on that EXACT demographic for your Facebook Ad.

Your potential customers are using Facebook…are YOU?

How to Publish Your First Ad – The Five Step Formula

Step 1: Getting Started

Go to: http://www.facebook.com/advertising.

Facebook Ads

Reach over 500 million people where they connect and share

Step 1: click on the 'Create An Ad Button'

Create an Ad

or manage your existing ads

Overview   Case Studies

Reach Your Target Customers
- Connect with more than 500 million potential customers
- Choose your audience by location, age and interests
- Test simple image and text-based ads and use what works

Deepen Your Relationships
- Promote your Facebook Page or website
- Use our "Like" button to increase your ad's influence
- Build a community around your business

Control Your Budget
- Set the daily budget you are comfortable with
- Adjust your daily budget at anytime
- Choose to pay only when people click (CPC) or see your ad (CPM)

After you click on the 'Create an Ad Button' you will see this screen:

I'll show you a 'REAL' ad we will place for driving traffic to a website – giving away a FREE report on real estate trends.

Note: *Free reports are a great "traffic magnet" to generate interest. You could also use free videos, webinar, events, white papers, and case studies.*

Second Note: *You can also drive traffic to your own Facebook Business Page if you have one.*

The above illustration shows you the
real live example of placing an ad.

Step 2: Targeting

Before we continue with the above example ad let me explain targeting.

To target all the users in the U.S., the estimated reach of over 120 million people!! Now as we all know, you'll get a better return on investment to target more close to where your customers are.

The analogy is this: You have a huge ocean to fish in, but you want to go to that one part of the ocean where the type of fish is that you want.

One of your main success activities should be how to target your market properly. There are several different factors you can use to narrow things down, including location targeting, education targeting, age targeting, keyword targeting, connection targeting, and sex targeting. It's kind of amazing!

You can target by location at the city level, radius level, country level, or state level. This super-location targeting makes the ads very effective for local businesses!

You can use education targeting down to where the person went or is going to school and even their major. Job targeting can work quite nicely as well, as you will find that those in certain industries will be most interested in your product or service. Again, it is in your best interest to learn everything you can about the market you are trying to sell to.

Relationship targeting is another interesting and important method. Perhaps your products or services are better geared towards people who are single. You can certainly make that distinction through Facebook ads. You can also target people who are engaged or already married. Do keep in mind that some people do not specify this information, and your ads will not appear to them if you choose to target based on the relationship category.

A relatively new feature is that you can target ads based on connections made within Facebook. This can include people who are attending certain events, those who "like" certain pages or things, and those who are using certain apps, and so on.

You can target keywords based on favorite TV shows, movies, occupation, hobbies, books, music, sports, and more. Consider what things your prospective customers like. Think about what really interests them the most, and target keywords based on that.

Note that you can even combine these different requirements for targeting down to incredible levels. For instance, you can target someone of a certain age, sex, marital status, and favorite book! It's almost scary how targeted these ads can become. It's definitely good for business, because as we all know having a message to market match is key. You won't be wasting money on people who will never be interested in what you have to offer.

So let's get back to our example ad:

After you hit the "Continue" button above...you will see the following screen:

Now the reach is over 120 million so let's target a bit more to where "the fish" are shall we? The next illustration shows how I entered:

- A city (Tampa)
- A radius of the city (within 25 miles of Tampa)
- Males between age 35 to 55
- Likes of 'travel' (typically my target market enjoys travelling)

And so now, the 'estimated reach' has gone from over 120 million to just over 7,000 as shown below:

Estimated Reach

7,080 people

- who live in the **United States**
- who live within 25 miles of **Tampa, FL**
- between the ages of **35** and **55** inclusive
- who are **male**
- who like **travel**

You will also have the ability to further target as shown below:

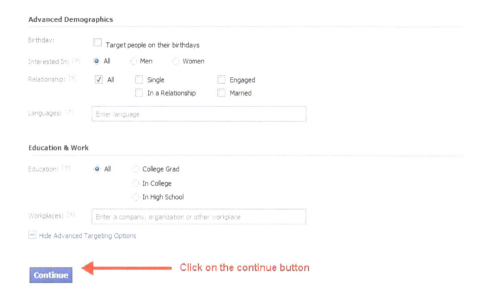

In this example, I won't select any of the options above but it shows you how "micro-targeted" you can get!

Step 3: Scheduling and Pricing Your Ad

Now you are at the step where you can decide when and for what price to advertise. It is a strong marketing suggestion that you already know "how much are you willing to pay for a lead".

For example, if 100 people click on your ad and 3 people end up buying what you have to offer...how much money do those 3 people bring into your business? As long as that number is greater than the cost of getting 100 clicks to your offer...then you have a sound business!

The image below shows what you see after you hit the 'Continue' button above:

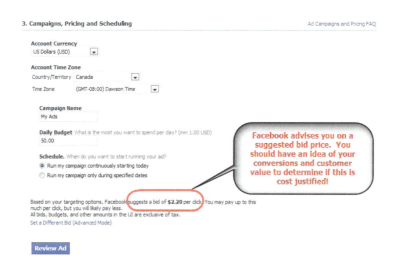

Step 4: Review Your Ad

After you hit the 'review ad' in step 3, you'll see the next screen
which is rather intuitive and you can either proceed or edit your ad.

 Review Ad
Please review your ad for accuracy.

Ad Preview:

**Totally FREE Trends
VIDEO**

How to buy Florida real
estate foreclosures and
profit wildly.

Maria Gudelis likes this ad.

👍 Like

Ad Name:	Totally FREE Trends VIDEO
Audience:	This ad targets users:
	▪ who live in the United States
	▪ who live within 25 miles of Tampa, FL
	▪ between the ages of 35 and 55 inclusive
	▪ who are male
	▪ who like travel
Campaign:	My Ads (New Campaign)
Bid Type:	CPC
Bid:	$2.20 USD per click
Daily Budget:	$50.00 USD per day
Duration:	This ad campaign will run indefinitely

[**Place Order**] [Edit Ad]

After you set up your payment method, you will see a screen similar
to the one below in this example.

> *Note: There is always a "waiting period" before your ad "goes live" so that Facebook can review your ad.*

Once your ad "goes live", you must follow step 5 so that you can maximize your Return on Investment. Additionally, you probably are savvy enough to know this...but DON'T FORGET about your ad...if you have set it up to run daily; it's up to you to stop running the ad!

So now the fun part begins...watching YOU get TRAFFIC to your site!

Facebook also allows you to "preview" what the ad looks like on your profile. That is a nice feature so you can see what it will look like for your target prospect. In this example, here is what the ad looks like on my profile:

Step 5: Testing and Tweaking for Maximum ROI

On the next nine pages, we'll cover what you need to do to build a foundation of testing and tweaking your Facebook ads.

I've included testing and tweaking as a specific STEP so that you don't forget to do this! It's that important. You wouldn't want to spend $100 per day sending traffic if you are not converting that traffic into a buyer or potential buyer who has "opted into" your email marketing system.

The way to maximize your Return on Investment (ROI) is to monitor how many people out of those one hundred prospects took the action you wanted? Is it 1.5%, 3%, 10% or ?????. You should know these numbers.

Why? Because then you can compare – if you change the 'headline', does the conversion go from 3% to 5%? That may seem like a small percentage but it can mean THOUSANDs in your pocket.

Let me explain, if the lifetime value of just ONE of your customers is $1,000...then 3 new customers is worth $3,000 to you right? So if you can increase your conversions **from 3% to 5%,** you just increased by two more customers and voila, you **have an additional $2,000 into your business!**

So read carefully the next section that will help you with testing and tracking!

Bonus: Ensuring Your Ad Stands Out

There are so many people moving to Facebook for advertising these days that you'll want to do everything in your power to ensure your ad stands out. You want people to click your ad so you can get more leads and make more sales!

That is part of the reason why doing market research is so important. You need to be able to "speak the language" of the people you are targeting with your ads. Figure out exactly how you can phrase your ad so the right people are attracted to it. Be as specific as you can be! Remember -- it's not about how many clicks you can get in general; it's about how many clicks you can get from those who will be most likely to buy from you.

While you want to be descriptive, you don't want to be long-winded. Make sure you use complete sentences that are well-written. Avoid using words that are unnecessary. You want your ad to be "punchy" and call out to your target audience. It's not a matter of stating everything you have to state right in the ad -- just enough so that people who are most likely to buy from you become interested and click on the ad.

That's part of why it's so important to include a great call-to-action. It's a very basic part of copywriting that is oh-so-essential! For example, you can tell people to "buy today" or "check out your limited-time only" sales. It's partly subliminal, but telling people exactly what they should do can definitely improve your results.

A very exciting feature of Facebook is that you can use images within your ads.

These can work very well! They allow images that are up to 100 pixels by 80 pixels. Match the image to what you are selling, and it can help your ad stand out and get more clicks from the right people. Faces naturally draw eyes, so it is a great idea to use them if it matches what you are promoting.

Using the Ads Manager

Facebook provides the Ad Manager to make it easy to set up and manage your ads. You can also optimize your ad for best performance, improve your targeting, and set your bids and budgets!

If you go to the Ads Manager, you'll find that it is very easy to use. The front page (once you have already signed up to get started) will let you to create an ad, receive any notifications, evaluate your spending per day, examine the status of your current ads, and evaluate performance based on graphs. It also allows you to search and browse, and, of course it has a great help area.

One of the favorite features is the other real-time metrics you can use to optimize your ads. Everything updates in real time -- which is a great improvement over other ad solutions. It's easy to find out exactly what is and is not working so you can tweak, pause or restart campaigns, and figure out exactly what you want your budget to be.

The ads manager starts off with the homepage, of course, which is sort of like a digest for everything related to your ads. There is also a campaign page that allows you to see more in-depth information about your campaigns.

The Ads Manager area targets everything a little bit more. You'll be able to preview your ad, edit the name, status, bids, and your methods of targeting. Go ahead and take some time to go through the ad manager area. The chances are very good you will find it is quite easy to use. It all happens here!

Landing Pages that Convert Like Crazy

Landing pages are a very important part of your ad. After all, even if you have a wonderful ad, you're certainly not going to make any sales if the landing page isn't relevant or well done! Make sure it fits seamlessly together with your ad. Make sure that anyone who is interested enough to click on your ad finds exactly what they were looking for when they arrive to your site.

For instance, if you're advertising something that is on a specific page of your website, you'll want to take people to that specific page rather than to a more general page on your site. This will help to increase your conversions.

Be aware that those who approve (or deny!) Facebook ads will be taking a look at your landing page. It absolutely must fit within their guidelines or you will not get your ad improved.

Your landing page should be pleasing to the eye. It should also be immediately obvious what people are supposed to do once they arrive to your page. Make it super-easy for people to buy from you, and you'll make a lot of sales. If you're not sure if you've done it right, have testers look at and explore your page so you can get an idea of how easy it is for others to use your site.

Making Changes to Dramatically Improve Your Ads

Any successful advertiser tracks their results and makes changes if necessary. Take a look at how your ads are performing. What is your click-through rate? Are people buying once they have clicked? If you're not making enough money to compensate for what you're spending on the ads, then things definitely have to change! No matter how well you think things are going, it's usually the case that a few tweaks here and there can dramatically improve your results.

Test and track different ads. That is the only way you'll know what will really work for you. It's easy to get lazy if something seems to be working -- or to give up right away if it doesn't work right away. The fact is that Facebook is an amazing advertising platform for a wide variety of markets, so it would be a shame not to take advantage of that.

Tracking Conversions

It is incredibly important to track your success through your advertisements. The good news is that Facebook provides you with many tools to do so! You can do this through the basic Ad Manager, and even download reports for further study.

A great feature of Facebook Ad Manager is the included conversion tracking. You'll be able to see what happens on your website after someone has clicked through to your landing page. This will help you to optimize and tweak your campaigns so they are as effective as possible. Obviously, the more conversions you are getting, the better!

To get started, you'll need to go to the tracking section of your Ad account. Facebook will have given you a tracking tag that is specific to your campaign. You can create new tracking tags as well for differing campaigns. You're able to name the tab, choose what it will track, and assign a value associated with the type of conversion. For example, it can tell you whether the person has made a purchase, signed up for your list, or participated in another activity that you have specified.

After you have set up your tracking tag, all you'll need to do is copy and paste the tag into your website's code. This will allow their system to determine what kind of conversions you are getting. You might enter different codes on different areas of your site, depending on which conversion you want to track.

Facebook can track many different kinds of conversion events! Examples include page views, purchases, download, registrations, and even page views that eventually lead to conversions.

Facebook will start generating reports for you after you have properly entered your conversion tags into your website. You will want to download reports based on advertising performance, responder demographics, and responder profiles. You can find this in the reports section of your Facebook Ads Manager.

It will track the conversions, post-impression and post-click data. It will give you information about how long it took from the time people saw your ad to when they clicked through. You will also have access to an advertising performance report that will show you just how effective your campaign is.

Of course, it's very important to understand what you should be looking for when you go through these reports and tools. You want to see how people are clicking, your click through rates, your cost per click, how many people are taking the desired action, and how many actions are being taken.

By analyzing this data, you can fully determine if your campaign is successful. In some cases, you may need to do a lot of tweaking because you're losing money. In other cases, you might find that you are doing quite well and that you are getting a lot of desired actions. It's all about conversions!

Improving Your Click-Through Rates

You might have heard some people complaining that Facebook's click-through rates are dismal compared to that of other pay per click companies. Pay no attention -- those who are not getting a very high click-through rate are simply not doing the right things!

You are going to need to put yourself in your potential customer's shoes. If you were them, what would make you want to click one of the ads on Facebook? Imagine yourself as a customer -- you are just

going about your business, checking people's status updates, looking at their photos, and so on. What would grab your attention?

You need to be able to create some sort of pattern interrupt that will get them to pause and see what you have to say. Even better -- you want them to go ahead and click your ad!

Go to your Facebook account right now and see what kind of ads people are putting up. What are they saying? What image have they posted along with their ad? If you hadn't been consciously thinking about ads, would you have clicked through? The chances are good that you would have completely ignored it!

On the flip side, have you ever been on Facebook when you DID click an ad? What was it that made you click? You may even want to keep a record of ads you see on Facebook that are great. Getting inspired by others is an easy way to come up with your own great ideas for ads.

Split Testing Your Ads

If you have ever advertised on Google Adwords before, then you're very familiar with split testing your ads. Facebook allows this functionality as well. You can create different versions of your ad to see how people in a certain demographic react to it. From there, you can tweak things to see what is performing better -- you can make better use of the money you're spending!

Using Facebook Ads as a Relationship Builder -- Really!

Facebook got its start as a way for people to connect socially. It has evolved into something much more, but at its heart it is still a social network that thrives on building relationships. That is why you'll have the most success if you have a presence on Facebook already.

In fact, there is evidence that having a fan page where people can "like" your company or your niche is a great way to attract people to your ads. The bottom line is that people are a lot more likely to connect to and appreciate a company they have heard of before.

This also has to do with how well you target. If your particular product or service is obviously geared toward a small group of people, it doesn't make sense to get greedy and go for more general targets just for the sake of clicks. You'll end up wasting a lot of money because the people who click through to your landing page (if they click at all) will not be a good match.

Interactive ads that build a relationship to a targeted group of people are where it's at! You can set up your ads so that they can RSVP to an event or "like" product or service directly from the advertisement. From there on out, you can communicate with them and really build a relationship with them.

That is why so many advertisers direct their visitors to another page on Facebook rather than to an off-page site. It shows up in friends' feeds when someone likes your page -- this is awesome exposure for you!

This type of marketing has similar qualities to building a list so you can e-mail market to people, except it's all done on Facebook. This is a great idea since Facebook has such a large reach!

Getting in Front of the Conversation

Social media has changed the face of advertising for everyone. It's not enough to just throw a banner ad up these days. You've got to get in front of the conversation in a marketplace. You need to get people to become engaged with your brand.

Nielson(http://blog.nielsen.com/nielsenwire/online_mobile/nielsenfacebook-ad-report) calls this "earned media." They measure the effectiveness of this in terms of brand awareness, message awareness, and purchase intent. You can get in front of the conversation to make your ads more effective. Get people interested in what you have to say, use social ads, and do what you can to spread the word about your product or service.

Interactive Ads like You've Never Seen Before

There are two different types of ads on Facebook. There's the regular Facebook Ad, which is more like your standard Google Adwords ad, and the social ad. The social ad ties the ads into actions people take when they see it -- we've touched on this already, but it bears repeating since it's such a fascinating advertising avenue. Facebook is able to use the action as enticement for you to do the same.

It is quite creative, and Facebook is certainly paving the way for interactive ads. Members can use comments on social ads. There are also virtual gift style ads that users can give to one another. Finally, users can "like" a certain company or product.

If a person "likes" a company or a product, it can show up in the feeds of others, leading to organic traffic to your offer as well! That means that a paid ad can pay off in more ways than with the individual who clicked on your ad.

This also has to do with relationship building -- if people are familiar with your brand and know that other people are as well (with a factor of trust), then they are a lot more likely to go ahead and engage with your company as well.

Nielson Media Research did a study (over a period of 6 months, surveying 800,000 Facebook users and 125 ad campaigns from 70 advertisers) which showed that homepage ad exposure alone did well -- but when it was combined with social advocacy, it greatly increased ad recall, awareness, and purchase intent. Recall grew from 10% to 16%, awareness grew from 4% to 8%, and purchase intent grew from 2% to 8%.

Clearly, it pays off to use these interactive ads and to build a relationship with users -- it attracts friends and family members! This type of advertising can definitely lead to you getting more exposure for your money.

Budgeting On Facebook

They are so many people who waste money advertising on Facebook because they do not understand how to budget! Don't just jump into advertising on Facebook without knowing what you are doing. Otherwise, you can end up wasting thousands of dollars with nothing to show for it.

Obviously, you want to make sales and get more customers. However, you need to have some clear goals in mind. First of all, do you want to try and make the sale right away? Or, do you want to build a relationship over time in hopes of getting even more sales in the future? In most cases, marketing on Facebook works best as a relationship builder so you can get more customers and sales in the long term.

Part of the problem in doing this is that you may not be sure you are actually engaging your customers. Stay on top of things when people are commenting on your page and "liking" what you have to offer. Sure to follow up with them frequently so that you see at the top of their minds. Doing this will accomplish a lot of things for your business!

The reason all of this was mentioned again in the "budgeting" section is because you'll want to dedicate part of your budget to building that relationship. You'll want to look at things both in terms of things like click-throughs and how your reach starts to grow organically through the power of Facebook.

You will find that as you start to get a higher click-through rate, you will pay less for your ads. Monitor your company's finances, and tweak things over time, and it will become even easier for you to budget.

Summary of Top Tips for Better Facebook Ads

By this point, you should have a pretty good idea of the fact that Facebook can be a very effective advertising tool for your business. There are some things that are important to reiterate in order to help you set up and optimize your ad campaign.

First, let's review tips on targeting. Matching your message to the market is absolutely critical. Really step into your customer's shoes to determine who you should be targeting. You can even do a little sleuthing! Consider what people who are searching for particular products (yours) are likely to include in their profiles so you can more easily target them.

Another thing you'll need to think about is when you are displaying your ads. In some cases, your ad might do incredibly well during one certain time of the year, and in other cases it will completely bomb.

Writing your ad copy is a really important part of the process. You want to make sure you're calling out the people you are targeting. Consider how they speak to one another. Do whatever you can to pique their interest. This can include making limited time offers, and more. A great way to improve your click through rates is to ask for what you want!

Facebook sets itself apart from other advertising networks because they allow you to put images up along with your ads. Be sure that they are highly relevant and eye-catching. Know that images of faces tend to draw eyes, and hopefully clicks.

On occasion, you might want to try different images in ad copy. Not only will this help you test and track, it will keep your advertisements fresh. That's because some of the same people might have already seen your ad, and a slightly different advertisement might get you that click!

Definitely consider sending your ads to your company's Facebook page. Then they can "like" your page and you can really go viral! You can take advantage of relationship marketing, which is highly effective and a lot more likely to get you a customer that can last for a lifetime.

Not only is your ad important -- what comes after the ad is just as important! Always keep in mind that your landing page should be optimized and highly targeted. People should find what they expect to find from reading your ad copy.

Facebook gives advertisers a lot of wonderful tools. Make sure you're making use of your reports so you can improve the effectiveness of your ads. You should get very used to testing your ads and tweaking them, because this is the best way to increase the amount of money you make and expand your reach from your advertisements!

A Special Note for Those Directing Ads to a Facebook Page

As we've discussed, one of the best strategies is to advertise your Facebook page. You'll definitely want to ensure that you have the manpower in place to manage this page. If possible, dedicate someone to be in control of posting new information, posting pictures, and more.

It is most important to frequently look at the Facebook page to answer people's questions, keep up with comments, and monitor activity. You should definitely have a strategy in place and keep your finger on the pulse of the marketplace for best results.

Go Make Some Money!

Advertising on Facebook is one of the best ways to get more business! Gone are the days where all you could do was put up a flashy banner ad and hope that someone would click on it. These days, you can super-target down to the finest levels. This allows you to optimize your campaigns very easily and ensure that you get more for your money.

Despite the fact that you have done the right thing by studying these materials, you may want to start off slowly when you begin advertising on Facebook. It's easy to lose your shirt when starting out with pay per click campaigns! Even those who are very experienced with Facebook ads have to take pause, study their reports, and optimize frequently.

Soon enough, you should find that your ads are very successful and that you are having a wonderful experience on Facebook. You're reaching those you need to reach, and developing relationships with those in your target market. There are no two ways about it -- advertising on Facebook is something that every company who pays for advertising should be doing! Every business, whether large or small, can benefit from this advertising method.

Take everything you've learned here and apply it to your ads today. You will be light years ahead of those who just decide to sign up one day and are not quite sure of what they should be doing. This puts you way ahead of your competition, which can do wonderful things for your business. Don't let self-doubt hold you back. Get out there and start advertising on Facebook!

Resources

Check out some other cool products that can add fast profits to your business:

Make Cash Fast with our FREE 90-Day Challenge at
www.CashNowChallenge.com

An Entire List of Maria's Products can be found at
www.MariaGudelisProducts.com

The following published books by Maria Gudelis and available on Amazon, Kindle, and Barnes and Noble:

21 Ways To Use Social Media

21 Ways To Use Social Media by Maria Gudelis: "Steal" These Ways To Maximum Social Media Success [Paperback]
Maria Gudelis ⊡ (Author)
★★★★★ ⊡ (13 customer reviews)

Price: **$17.00** & eligible for **FREE Super Saver Shipping** on orders over $25. Details
In Stock.
Ships from and sold by **Amazon.com.** Gift-wrap available.

Want it delivered Tuesday, May 11? Order it in the next 16 hours and 33 minutes, and choose **One-Day Shipping** at checkout. Details

The Twitter Business Advantage – How Small Businesses Can use Twitter as the Perfect Sales Machine

The Twitter Business Advantage. KLT. Building your Business around the Clock with Twitter's Know, Like, Trust Factor (Volume 1) [Paperback]
Ms. Tina Williams (Author), Maria Gudelis (Contributor), Mr. Art Nevarez (Contributor)
★★★★★ ▾ (1 customer review)

Price: **$17.00** & eligible for **FREE Super Saver Shipping** on orders over $25. Details

In Stock.
Ships from and sold by **Amazon.com**. Gift-wrap available.

Want it delivered Tuesday, May 11? Order it in the next 16 hours and 29 minutes, and choose **One-Day Shipping** at checkout. Details

Speak for Profits Now: YOUR 7 Step Action Plan to Get LIVE Speaking Gigs with Chambers and Other Groups

7 Step Action Plan: Get LIVE Speaking Gigs with Chambers and Other Groups [Paperback]
Ms. Maria Gudelis (Author)
★★★★★ ▾ (2 customer reviews)

Price: **$17.00** & eligible for **FREE Super Saver Shipping** on orders over $25. Details

In Stock.
Ships from and sold by **Amazon.com**. Gift-wrap available.

Want it delivered Tuesday, May 11? Order it in the next 16 hours and 24 minutes, and choose **One-Day Shipping** at checkout. Details

Notes:

www.ingramcontent.com/pod-product-compliance
Lightning Source LLC
Chambersburg PA
CBHW041146050326
40689CB00001B/509